ALFRED'S Solo Spectacular!

LATE ELEMENTARY TO EARLY INTERMEDIATE PIANO SOLOS

By FAVORITE ALFRED COMPOSERS   BOOK 2

There is something magical about a sheet music solo. Give your students a new solo and watch their eyes sparkle! Over the years, sheet music solos have proven to be motivating, rewarding and exciting for students of all ages.

The magic of sheet music continues in Alfred's Solo Spectacular! series. Available in three separate collections, you will find some of our best-loved sheet music solos by your favorite Alfred composers including Dennis Alexander, Cynthia Sepaugh Clarke, Margaret Goldston, Randall Hartsell, David Karp, Gayle Kowalchyk, E. L. Lancaster, Martha Mier, June C. Montgomery, Lynn Freeman Olson and Catherine Rollin.

Give your students something magical. Give them a sheet music collection from Alfred.

Caribbean Breeze (Lynn Freeman Olson) 10

Fiddle Tune (Martha Mier) 14

Fire Dance (David Karp) 8

Isle of Palms (Randall Hartsell) 16

I Want My Mummy! (Margaret Goldston) 2

Jazz Hound (Catherine Rollin) 12

Prelude Majestic (Margaret Goldston) 22

Secret Agent of the 88s (Catherine Rollin) 19

Three-Legged Witch, The (Dennis Alexander) 4

Tough Cookie! (Dennis Alexander) 6

Alfred

Cover photo: © Mark Drewelow/Stock Imagery   Cover design: Carol Kascsak
Music engraving: Nancy Butler

I Want My Mummy!

Margaret Goldston

With spirit!

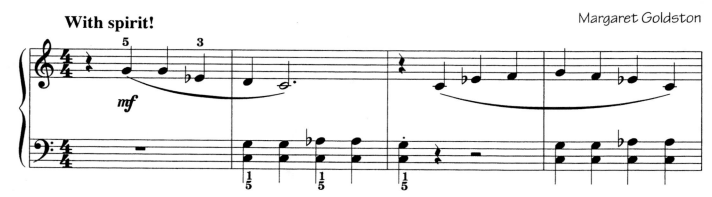

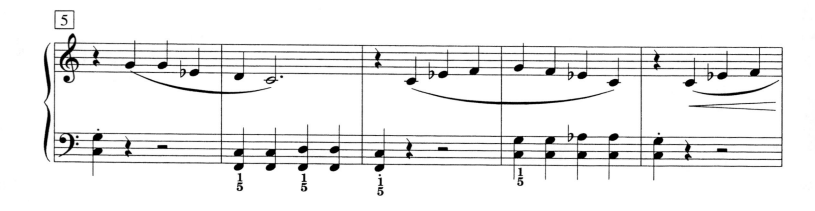

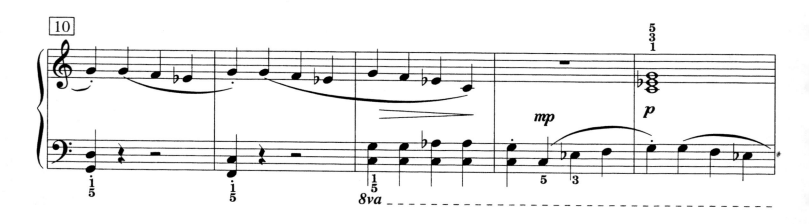

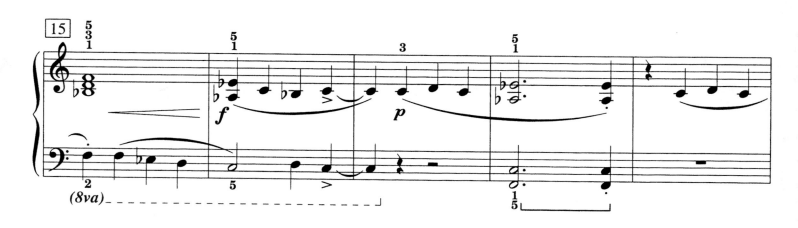

The Three-Legged Witch

Andante

Dennis Alexander

Can you hear in the bush - es near, all the three - leg - ged

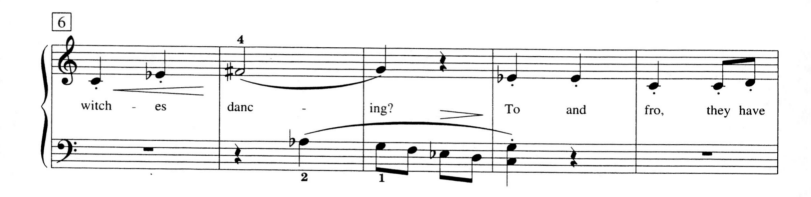

witch - es danc - ing? To and fro, they have

fif - teen toes, and three legs which go "Ker - plunk,

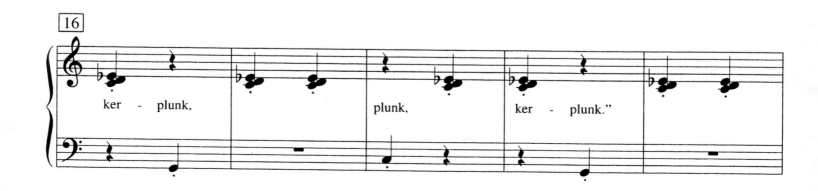

ker - plunk, plunk, ker - plunk."

5

Tough Cookie!

Dennis Alexander

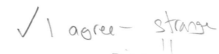

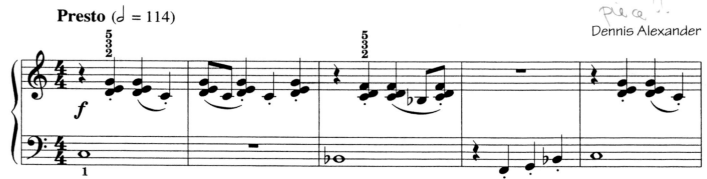

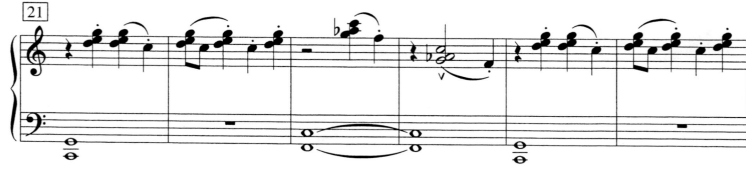

for Adam Ratner

Fire Dance

David Karp

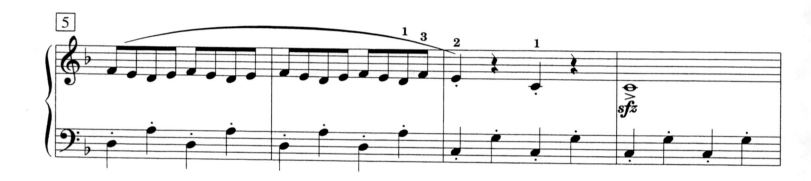

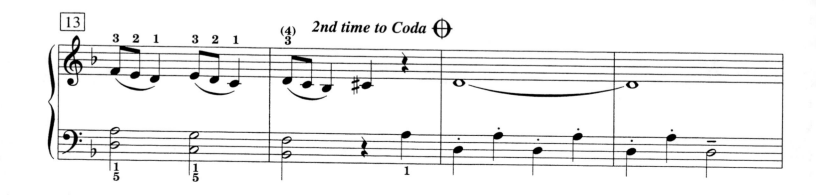

Caribbean Breeze

Lynn Freeman Olson

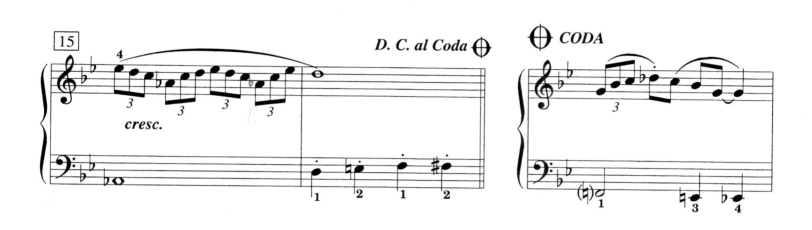

Fiddle Tune

Martha Mier

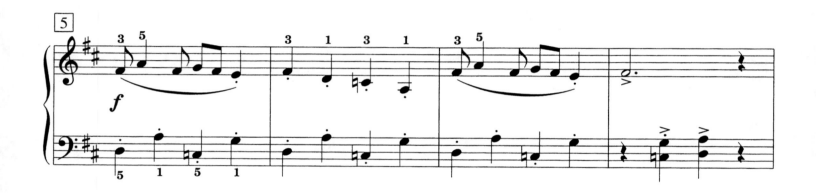

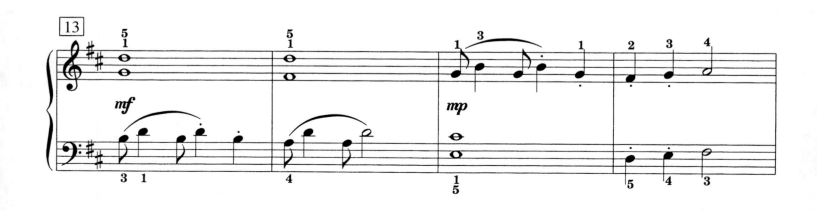

Isle of Palms

yes and we don't like it!

Randall Hartsell

Secret Agent of the 88s

Very good

Catherine Rollin

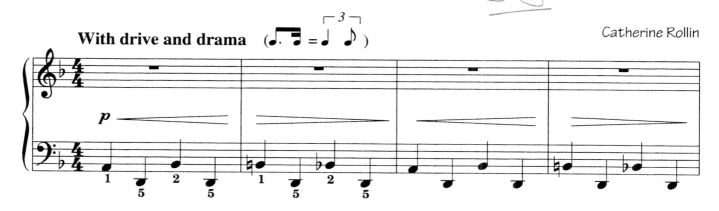

to Coda ⊕

Prelude Majestic

(Variations on a Ground Bass*)

Margaret Goldston

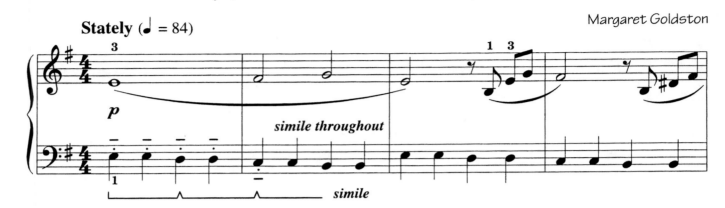

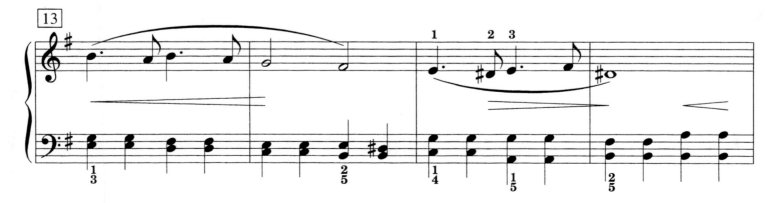

*A "ground bass" is a continually repeating pattern in the bass accompaniment.
   In this prelude it is two measures long.